Dear Boys and Girls:

Squanto, the Wampanoag, belonged to a tribe that is related to mine by language. I am a Sauk. He spoke Algonquian Indian languages, as I do. But we could not understand each other if Squanto were alive today to talk to me.

Instead, we would have to speak English. Squanto learned your language from the sailors, adventurers and Pilgrims who landed in Massachusetts. I learned mine in school when I was growing up.

Squanto was the first Indian to make friends with the Pilgrim Fathers. He taught them how to plant corn, beans and squash, how to trap eels, and how to travel through the woods.

Squanto's life was one of peace and helpfulness to all men. We can all learn a great deal from studying it.

Sincerely,

George W. Harris

George W. Harris
Sauk Indian
Descendant of Chief
Grey Eyes

SQUANTO
INDIAN ADVENTURER

BY STEWART AND POLLY ANNE GRAFF

ILLUSTRATED BY ROBERT DOREMUS

GARRARD PUBLISHING COMPANY
CHAMPAIGN, ILLINOIS

This book is for
LIB GRAFF
with the authors' love

ALICE MARRIOTT and CAROL K. RACHLIN of Southwest Research Associates are consultants for Garrard Indian Books.

MISS MARRIOTT has lived among the Kiowa and Cheyenne Indians in Oklahoma and spent many years with the Pueblos of New Mexico and the Hopis of Arizona. First woman to take a degree in anthropology from the University of Oklahoma, she is a Fellow of the American Anthropological Association, now working with its Curriculum Project.

MISS RACHLIN, also a Fellow of AAA and of the American Association for the Advancement of Science, is a graduate in anthropology of Columbia University. She has done archaeological work in New Jersey and Indiana, and ethnological field work with Algonquian tribes of the Midwest.

Contents

1 The Strangers 7

2 New Friends 13

3 New Adventure 19

4 Kidnapped 25

5 Escape 33

6 The Rescue 41

7 Plymouth 47

8 Hobomok 54

9 The Snakeskin 63

10 Trouble 71

11 The Last Trip 77

Wampanoag Indians

The Wampanoag Indians, of which Squanto was a member, were a tribe of the Algonquins. These peaceful Indians lived in the woodlands of Massachusetts and Rhode Island, mostly along the coast. They lived in dome-shaped wigwams made of bent young trees faced with plants or birch bark. They hunted, fished, gathered berries and nuts, and they liked to sing and play games.

It was the Wampanoags who helped the Pilgrims. They taught them how to live in the woods, find food and plant corn.

Massasoit, the Wampanoags' chief, made a peace treaty with the Pilgrims, which he kept as long as he lived.

These Indians called the deer, the fish and the turtle their brothers. They worshipped nature and believed their dreams were sent by their god, to guide and help them.

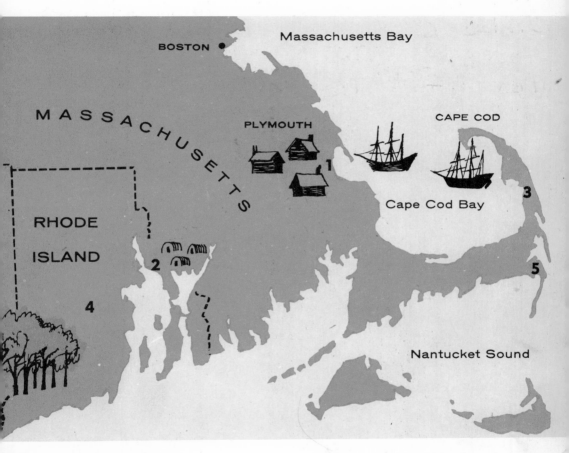

1. Plymouth was built where Squanto's village, Patuxet, had been located.

2. Chief Massasoit had his headquarters here when he received his red coat from the Pilgrims.

3. The friendly Nauset Indians lived in this area.

4. Canonicus' tribe, the Narragansetts, lived in this area.

5. Squanto's last trip ended here. He died in 1622 near what is now Chatham, Massachusetts.

1

The Strangers

The October woods smelled spicy and good. Pine needles made a soft, brown carpet. An Indian boy and his dog moved swiftly along the trail. The boy's name was Squanto.

It was the long-ago year of 1612. Squanto was a Wampanoag Indian. He lived with his family in the Indian village of Patuxet on the shore of Massachusetts Bay.

Squanto's father had taught him to hunt. His arrows shot swift and true. Squanto had learned to trap beavers and muskrats. His father had taught him other important things. He must not show pain when he was hurt. And he must never show fear.

The Indians had no calendar. Squanto did not know what year he had been born. He did not know his birthday. But he could count. He knew he had lived fourteen summers. His shoulders were thin, but he was strong.

"He will be a tall man," his mother said.

This afternoon Squanto had come a long way from home. He liked to hunt in a meadow near the sea. There were always wild birds there. As Squanto walked out of the dark woods, he heard a whirr of wings. In an instant Squanto's bow was drawn. His arrow shot. The bird fluttered and dropped.

"I will take it home for supper," Squanto said to himself. He did not have to hurry. The sun was still high. He whistled to his dog, Canjo. "Let's hunt for clams," he said. "I'm hungry."

He raced Canjo down the beach. Suddenly, as they rounded a point, Squanto stopped. A strange ship floated in the blue water of the cove. It was the biggest ship Squanto had ever seen. "It is like an island that moves," he thought in wonder.

He knew the ship must belong to traders. He had heard of the strangers who came from across the sea to trade with the Indians. Squanto's father did not trust the strangers. "The white men have sticks that roar and kill. Never go near them," he warned. "Our chief has forbidden it."

The next moment Squanto's heart thumped. Men from the ship were moving about a campfire on the beach.

Squanto knew he should hurry home and warn his father. But he was curious. He dropped into the beach grass and crept closer. Canjo crept at his heels. Squanto could hear the men talking in words that he could not understand. The men wore strange, heavy clothes. Even their heads were covered.

One of the men turned. Squanto could see the long stick in his hand.

10

Squanto lay very still. When the man turned back to the fire, Squanto motioned to Canjo. Silently, they moved into the woods and ran.

It was nearly dark when Squanto reached home. He ran to the campfire. "Father—" he began eagerly. Then he stopped. If he told about the strangers, his father would not let him go back to the cove. Squanto knew he wanted to see the strangers again. He stood quiet. Then he said, "Father, I brought home a bird to eat."

His father looked at the bird carefully. Then he looked at the boy. "You have shot well, my son," he said. "But why have you held the bird so tightly?"

2

New Friends

The next day Squanto hurried through his work and whistled for Canjo. They took a shortcut through the woods. Squanto carried two soft beaver skins with him. He moved carefully as he came near the cove.

The strangers were still there. They were cooking something over the fire.

Squanto was excited, but he did not feel afraid. Boldly, he walked toward them. One of the men saw him and called to the others. In a moment their long sticks were pointed toward him.

Squanto stood still. How could he tell them he was a friend? He called the Indian word for peace. The men did not understand. Squanto tried again. He held up the two beaver skins.

Slowly the men lowered their sticks. They beckoned to him and Squanto went toward them. He bowed politely. The strangers nodded back. They gave him a bowl of good-smelling stew. When he had finished eating, he patted his stomach. The men smiled.

They pointed to their leader and said, "Captain Weymouth."

Squanto repeated carefully, "Cap-tain.
Cap-tain." He pointed south toward
his home. "Patuxet," he said. And then,
"Wampanoag." The men understood.
They pointed across the wide ocean.
"England," they said.

"Eng-land," Squanto repeated. He
pointed to other things. He learned
more English words. "Dish. Spoon.

Man. Boat. Fire. Water—." The men pointed to the long sticks: "Gun." They pointed to Canjo: "Dog." Squanto said each word carefully.

Squanto was happy. He had new friends from a faraway country. When he left, the traders gave him some blue beads and a shiny knife. Squanto made signs that he would come back.

That night Squanto lay awake. The Indians were singing themselves to sleep. *"Eng-land,"* he whispered to himself. *"Eng-land."*

3

New Adventure

Late in the night Squanto woke suddenly. His father was shaking him. "Get up," his father said. "The chief has sent for you."

Squanto was bewildered. He followed his father to the chief's house. The chief and his council were waiting. "Squanto," the chief frowned angrily, "one of our scouts has seen strange white men on the shore to the north.

He saw you talking to these men and taking gifts from them. Is this true?"

Squanto faced the chief bravely. "It is true," he said. "The men come from a place called *Eng-land*. It is somewhere beyond the sea. They gave me food. They taught me some of their words."

"You have disobeyed." The chief's voice was like thunder. "We have warned you against strangers."

Squanto knew he had done wrong, yet he was not ashamed. He wanted to explain about the white men. Finally he spoke. "Would you come to meet the strangers?" he asked bravely. "They are friendly people. If you bring fur skins, they will trade knives with shining blades and many other things."

The chief and his elders still looked angry. "Go to your house, Squanto," one said. "Do not leave until we call."

Squanto thought they were deciding how to punish him. He tried to wait patiently. At last the chief sent for him. "We will go to trade with the strangers today," he said. "You will guide us."

Squanto wanted to shout with excitement, but he knew he must not show his joy. He bowed politely.

Later Squanto led them to the cove. The chief touched his shoulder. "Go," he said. "Say the Wampanoags bring peace."

Soon the Indians and the white men were seated around a big box. Captain Weymouth gave an order and his men opened the lid. The Indians' eyes

21

glistened when they saw the treasures inside. The trading began.

During the following days Squanto visited his new friends often. One afternoon he found them packing to leave. They would trade farther up the coast. When they had all the furs their ship could carry, they would sail over the great ocean to England.

Squanto was sad. "You come back?" he asked Captain Weymouth.

"Someday perhaps," the captain shrugged. Then he said, "Squanto, come with us. You can help us trade. Then we will take you to England."

Squanto's head felt dizzy. He wanted to go more than anything in the world. Yet how could he leave his family and people? Walking home, Squanto's feet dragged. But when he saw his family he spoke quickly. "The white men are leaving tomorrow. They want me to go to England with them. I want to go."

Squanto's mother spoke bravely. "You were bound to go someday, my son," she said. "You were born to adventure."

Only Canjo whined sadly the next morning, when Squanto put his few belongings into his pack and started toward the rising sun.

4

Kidnapped

That night the fog was like a ghost over the sea. The ship's timbers creaked and the wind blew in the sails with a lonesome sound. Squanto was homesick. But during the busy days he did not have time to feel lonely.

When they stopped along the coast, Squanto rowed ashore with the men. He helped them make camp. He could build a fire quickly. He showed the men how his mother roasted meat. He

took his bow and arrow and hunted.

Squanto helped with the trading. He would lead the way into an Indian village and speak first. He told the Indians the white men meant no harm. They only wanted to trade.

Finally the ship started back to England. The weeks at sea were long. Squanto wondered if he would ever see his home again.

The traders' ship docked at last. When Squanto saw the great city of London, his eyes opened wide. Instead of woods and meadows, he saw rows of houses. People crowded the streets. Wagons and carriages rumbled over cobblestones. Peddlers shouted. Church bells rang. A great clock boomed the hour. Squanto put his hands over his

ears. "There is so much noise I cannot hear," he said.

One of his sailor friends laughed. "Come home with me," he said. "My family will give you supper and a bit of quiet." Squanto found a welcome with the sailor's family.

Squanto worked hard for Captain Weymouth. He learned to find his way about London. He saw the palace where the king lived. He walked over London Bridge that crossed the wide Thames River. Soon he could follow the city streets as easily as the trails in his woods at home.

Many months passed. Squanto made new friends. But he began to wish he could go home to his own people.

One morning Captain Weymouth told Squanto that Captain John Smith was sailing for America to explore near Massachusetts Bay.

Squanto's eyes flashed with excitement. "I will ask for work on his crew," he said eagerly. He hurried to the docks and found Captain Smith. His men were already loading the ship.

"Please, sir," Squanto said, "my home

is on Massachusetts Bay. I want to go back. I will do any work."

Squanto was a strong young man now. Captain Smith nodded. "I need another good hand. Tell the men to put you to work."

Squanto helped to load cargo. He learned that Captain Smith was taking two ships. Captain Hunt would be the master of the second. "You are lucky not to work for Captain Hunt," the sailors said. "He is a very hard master."

Squanto agreed. He did not like Captain Hunt's eyes. They were mean and shifty.

The voyage was fair. Squanto liked working for Captain Smith. The Captain asked Squanto many questions about his home. He wanted to know about the harbors and the tides and which Indians were friendly.

They anchored in Massachusetts Bay. Squanto knew he was near home.

Captain Hunt took his men ashore to trade. But Captain Smith wanted to sail along the coast and make maps. He asked Squanto to help. Squanto shook his head. "I must go home," he said. "I have been away too long."

Captain Smith understood. He pointed the way and Squanto started down the shore. Soon he was on a trail he knew.

Suddenly there was a shout from the beach behind him. Squanto stopped. He looked around and saw a man beckoning. It was Captain Hunt. Squanto did not want to go back, but the Captain was signaling for help.

Squanto turned. The next moment
two men jumped out of the bushes.
Strong hands held him. He struggled,
but he felt a cold knife against his
throat. He knew it was hopeless.
Captain Hunt had tricked him.

Squanto had been kidnapped.

5

Escape

Squanto's hands were tied. He was thrown into the ship's hold. There was only darkness. After a moment, Squanto heard someone breathing. Then he heard a groan. Squanto spoke an Indian word softly. A voice answered, and then another. There were other prisoners.

That night more were brought in. They were all Indians who had been captured by Captain Hunt. "We do not know where we are being taken," they said. "We cannot understand the white men's words."

"I will try to find out," Squanto said.

When a sailor brought them thin soup and bread to eat, Squanto asked him in English, "What will become of us?"

"Captain Hunt will take you to Spain," the sailor said. "There you will be sold as slaves."

Squanto clenched his fists in despair. He had been nearly home. Now every hour was taking him farther away. This time it might be forever. He tried to coax the sailor to help the prisoners escape.

The sailor shook his head. "I dare not help you," he answered. "None of

Captain Hunt's men like this business. But we are afraid of him. He would kill anyone who disobeys."

The time passed slowly. Sometimes the sailor loosened the prisoners' chains so they could move. Sometimes he brought them extra bits of food he had stolen from the galley. Still they grew thin.

When the ship landed, the prisoners were led off. Squanto blinked in the bright, hot sun. Spain was a country very different from England.

The next day the Indians were put on a platform in the marketplace. People shouted all around them. One by one, the Indians were led away by their new masters. Squanto was the last to be sold. He was still weak from the long imprisonment, but his voice roared above the crowd. "I am not a slave. I am a free man. Help me!"

Most of the people did not understand English. Many laughed. But Squanto saw three men in long, brown robes and hoods hurry to the platform. They argued with the man selling the Indians. Finally they led Squanto away.

The men who had saved Squanto were religious men, called monks. The monks told him they believed slavery was wrong. They were kind to Squanto. He worked in their sunny garden. It was good to feel strong again.

"We would like to help you get home," the monks told Squanto, "but America is very far away. Few ships go there. Perhaps we can put you on a ship to England."

One evening the oldest monk sent for Squanto. "A ship sails for England tomorrow," he said. "The sailors will take you aboard. We will miss you, my son."

Squanto was happy to see London again. He found some of his old friends. A man named John Slaney gave him work. Squanto took care of Mr. Slaney's horses. "We will help you find a ship going to America," Mr. Slaney said.

Finally Squanto sailed on a trading ship to Newfoundland. This was a large island far to the north of Squanto's home. He hoped the ship would travel down the coast to Massachusetts Bay. Instead it went back to England.

Squanto sailed on other trading ships. But none of them went near his home.

Squanto waited patiently. In 1619 he sailed with a trader named Captain Dermer. The ship moved smoothly over the wide sea. "We are going to land in Massachusetts Bay," Captain Dermer told Squanto.

Squanto looked happily at the sails

billowing in the winds. "Thank you, my friends the winds," he said softly. One morning he heard the welcome words: "Land ho!"

Squanto ran along the trail toward Patuxet. He had kept his promise. He had come back. He came around the last bend and raced toward the village. He started to call, "Mother, Father—"

Then he stopped. The village was silent. Squanto ran from house to house calling. No one answered. The houses were cold and empty. Only a squirrel chattered in a tree.

Squanto's eyes grew round with horror. The village was dead. His people, his family were gone.

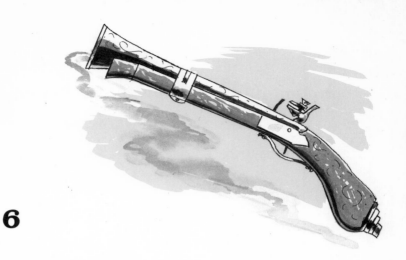

6

The Rescue

At first Squanto stood frozen with shock. Then he knew he must find out what had happened to his people. There were other Indians to the west. Perhaps they would know the answer.

Squanto hurried over the miles. When he saw campfire smoke he began to run. The Indians told him terrible news. Two summers before a great sickness had come to the Indians at Patuxet. They had almost all died.

Squanto listened, his head bowed.

"What will you do now, Squanto?" the Chief asked.

"I do not know," Squanto answered sadly. "I will go back to the English captain. I will work for him until I know what to do."

Squanto sailed with Captain Dermer's ship along the coast, stopping to trade. Squanto kept busy. He tried not to think about his lost family.

One day they came into a strange harbor. Captain Dermer and one of his sailors went ashore to look for water. Squanto waited with the others in the boat. Soon the sailor came running back. His clothes were torn. "Captain Dermer has been captured by Indians," he gasped. "Hurry! Help him!"

The men jumped up. Squanto shook his head. "Let me go alone," he said.

Squanto walked boldly into the circle of Indians. Captain Dermer's hands were tied behind his back. Squanto looked hard at the Indians. Then he spoke. "I am Squanto. Why do you treat my friend this way?"

The Indians stood still. Squanto spoke again. "My father was a Wampanoag. Our tribe is great. The people in my village died of sickness two summers ago. But I did not die. I found a way to trap the sickness. I keep it in the ground. Now I can make it work against my enemies."

Squanto saw the Indians look at each other. Quickly he picked up Captain Dermer's gun. "I know the magic of

the white man's fire stick," he said. He lifted the gun high in the air and fired. There was a loud roar.

The Indians stood, unable to move. Squanto said, "Now untie my friend. And go in peace."

The Indians were afraid of Squanto's powers. They untied Captain Dermer and moved away silently into the woods.

"You saved my life," Captain Dermer told Squanto later. "I am sailing south to trade with the English colony in Virginia. Come with me."

"Thank you," said Squanto. "But I have traveled long enough. Massasoit is chief of all the Wampanoags. His village is near my old home. I am going to live there."

7

Plymouth

Squanto was happy to be with Indian people again. Once more he watched the swift dances in the leaping firelight. Once more he heard the stories of the great warriors and the strong hunters of his tribe. But he could not forget that he had traveled far and done many things in strange lands.

One night Squanto lay in his bed listening to the steady humming through the village as the Indians sang themselves to sleep. He had often been homesick for that sound. Now he turned restlessly. His thoughts went far away to the crowded streets of London and the days of adventure with the trading ships. He loved his people, but he knew he needed something more.

Squanto liked to talk in English with another young Indian in Massasoit's village. This Indian was named Samoset. He had come from a tribe to the north. He had learned some English words from traders. Squanto and Samoset became friends.

One warm day in March, 1621, Samoset returned from a visit to another

Indian village. He ran to find Squanto. "I came home by the shore trail," he said excitedly. "I saw a settlement of English people. They are building houses in the old village of Patuxet. Now they call it *Plymouth*. These men are not traders. They want to live here!"

"We must tell Massasoit at once," Squanto said.

The great chief listened. "We will visit these strangers and tell them we wish to be friendly," he said. "You must speak for us in English, Squanto."

When they came to the settlement, Squanto saw that the new people had built their houses where the Indian village had stood. "It is like seeing my old village alive again," he thought.

Captain Miles Standish met the

Indians. He was a short man with reddish hair. He had been a soldier in England. "Our leader is ready to welcome you," he said.

There was a roll of drums and then Governor Carver appeared. He looked at Massasoit and his tall braves. They had painted their faces. The chief wore beads around his neck.

Squanto introduced his chief. Governor
Carver bowed. "We wish to be your
friends," he said.

Squanto told Massasoit what the
Governor's words meant. Massasoit
nodded. Squanto spoke first in the
Indian language and then in the white
man's language. The Indians and the
settlers made an agreement, or *treaty*.

They promised that neither side would make war on the other. Neither would steal from the other. If an enemy attacked, they would fight the enemy together.

The rules were fair for both sides. The treaty was kept for many years.

Before Massasoit left, he invited the white men to visit his village. "Squanto will guide you," he said.

Squanto stayed in Plymouth and waited for the settlers to make the journey. He learned that they were called Pilgrims. They had come from England on a ship called the *Mayflower*. During the winter there had been much sickness. Many Pilgrims had died. Squanto saw that the ones who had lived looked pale and thin. There was not enough food. Still they were working bravely to build a new colony.

When it was time for the visit, the Pilgrims took presents for Massasoit. Squanto led them into the Indian village. They gave Chief Massasoit a bright red coat. He wore it proudly.

Before the Pilgrims left, Squanto spoke to Massasoit. "Long ago in London when I was a stranger, the English were my friends," he said. "Now these English people are strangers in a new country. I can help them. I want to stay in Plymouth."

8

Hobomok

"We are grateful to have you here," one of the Pilgrim leaders said to Squanto. His name was William Bradford. He worked hard and carefully. Squanto saw that the others brought their questions to him. Squanto and Bradford were soon very good friends. And Squanto went to live in Bradford's house.

"You can teach us many things," Bradford told Squanto. "We have never lived in a wilderness. We do not know how to find food or what crops to plant."

Squanto showed the men how to fish for cod and bass and how to hunt deer and birds. He told them which trees had strong, hard wood. He showed them which fields were best for planting. He taught them to trap for furs.

Young Johnny Billington and the other Pilgrim boys were proud to have an Indian brave for their friend. They followed Squanto deep into the woods when he set his traps. "But you must never come here alone," Squanto warned them.

On the first warm day, Squanto took

the boys to the Town Brook. They took off their shoes and stockings. "Tramp in the mud like this," Squanto said. Suddenly a fat, black thing moved quickly up out of the mud. Squanto moved even faster and caught it.

The boys scrambled back on the bank. Squanto laughed. "It is an eel," he said. "It is good to eat."

Young Johnny's eyes danced with mischief. "Let's take it home to my mother," he said. "She will think it is a snake."

Johnny was right. His mother did not like the long, black, slippery eel. But when Squanto cooked the meat it tasted good. "We should have trusted you, Squanto," she said.

The Pilgrims learned to trust Squanto

for many other things. He knew where to dig clams in the wet sand and which berries and nuts were good to eat. He led them on trading trips to Indian camps along the shore.

Squanto learned new things too. He listened when the Pilgrim children studied from their hornbooks. Johnny showed him the letters. "Here is S-Q-U-A-N-T-O" he said. "That spells your name." Squanto was pleased.

The spring days had come. Birds sang again. The ground was warm. "It is time to plant," Squanto said. He showed the Pilgrims how to plant Indian corn in hills. He put some small fish into each hill. "The fish will make food for the corn to grow," he said.

While they were planting, Governor

Carver became ill and died. William Bradford was elected to be the new Governor. Squanto felt proud to be living in the Governor's house.

One summer evening Squanto took his turn at guard duty on the hill. He saw Captain Standish returning with an exploring party. Squanto was surprised to see a young Indian brave walking beside the captain. Later the Indian told Squanto that his name was Hobomok. He was a Wampanoag from a village to the west.

"I have come to live with the white men too," Hobomok said. "I will help Captain Standish. He has already taught me words in English."

"You will be welcome here," Squanto said. He was glad to have an Indian

friend. He was pleased when the Governor asked Hobomok to come on the next trading trip.

But Hobomok did not like it when Squanto led the traders into the Indian camps. "I can speak English," he told Squanto. "The Governor should let me lead too."

Squanto did not answer. He went about his work and paid no attention to Hobomok's grumbling.

When they returned from the trading trip, they found Plymouth in great alarm. Johnny Billington had gone into the woods alone. He had not come back. "He may have been kidnapped," his mother wept.

Governor Bradford sent Squanto to Chief Massasoit. "Find out if he knows what happened to Johnny," he ordered.

Squanto hurried back to Plymouth with a message. Johnny had not been kidnapped. He had been lost. A group of Nauset Indians had rescued him. Johnny could not tell where Plymouth was so they took him to their village on Cape Cod, across Massachusetts Bay.

"We must sail to fetch him home," Governor Bradford told Squanto.

They found young Johnny safe and well. The Nauset Indians had learned that the white settlers were friendly. They hung strings of wampum around Johnny's neck. He felt like a hero.

Squanto frowned at Johnny in the boat going home. "It is not being a hero to get lost and worry people," he said. But he was glad to have Johnny back.

9

The Snakeskin

Autumn came. The harvest was finished. The Pilgrims' storehouse was filled with barrels of corn and barley and dried fish. Piles of wood were stacked for the winter fires. Beaver skins were stretched to dry. The woods were full of deer and wild game. In the cool nights, the bright hunter's moon shone in the sky.

"We are grateful for this bounty," Governor Bradford said. "We will have a feast of thanksgiving and ask our Indian friends to share it with us."

Squanto went to invite Massasoit. The chief came, bringing 90 Indians. Squanto was proud to show them the Pilgrim village. For the great feast there were platters of roast duck and turkey and lobster. The women brought bowls of nuts and sweet grapes.

Massasoit saw there was still not enough food for so many Indian guests. He sent his hunters to shoot deer for more meat. Everyone sat outdoors to eat. The midday sun was warm. The men had shooting contests with guns and bows and arrows. The children played on the shore.

The Indians stayed three days. Before they said good-bye, everyone stood together with heads bowed. Elder Brewster prayed for another year of peace and plenty.

A few weeks later, an English ship, the *Fortune*, brought 35 new settlers. The Pilgrims shared their food and their small houses with the newcomers.

Winter came early. One snowy day in December Squanto came back from a hunting trip. When he reached the Town Brook, Johnny ran to meet him. The boy's eyes were wide. "A strange message has come from some Indians," Johnny said. "No one knows what it means."

The whole village was waiting for Squanto. He hurried to see Governor

Bradford and Captain Standish. They showed him a rattlesnake skin filled with Indian arrows. It had been left near the settlement. "What does it mean?" they asked Squanto.

Squanto knew. "It is a warning from the Narragansetts," he said. "They are a fierce tribe to the southwest. Their chief, Canonicus, would like to capture Massasoit's tribe. He wants to make war on Plymouth because the white men are Massasoit's friends. You must answer the warning."

"But how?" the Governor asked.

"Show them you have something more dangerous than arrows," Squanto said. "Fill the snakeskin with gunpowder and bullets and return it to Canonicus."

They filled the skin. Two scouts carried it back to the Narragansett chief.

The Pilgrims waited anxiously for an answer. They were afraid the Indians might attack.

A long night passed and then another.

Just as a pale sun was rising, the two scouts came limping out of the snowy woods. Their feet were half frozen from traveling miles over the icy ground. "We gave the snakeskin to Canonicus," they told Governor Bradford. "The chief would not touch it. His elders were frightened."

A few days later the snakeskin with powder and bullets was found nailed to a tree near Plymouth. It meant the Narragansetts would not attack the Pilgrims.

Squanto's message had saved them.

10

Trouble

The winter of 1622 was long. By spring the storehouse was nearly empty. With extra people to feed, Governor Bradford was worried. He sent Squanto to an Indian village to trade for corn.

Hobomok complained to the Governor. "Why didn't you send me?"

"There is plenty of work for you here," Governor Bradford answered sharply. "We will start planting tomorrow."

Through the spring days the whole colony worked together. The boys cut wood and brought boatloads of codfish to salt and dry. The women and girls helped plant and hoe the fields. The youngest children weeded the rows of beans and corn.

Squanto worked with the men who were building a fort and walls to protect the colony. They cut and dragged heavy logs. "We do not want war with anyone," the Governor said, "but if danger comes, we must defend ourselves."

Only a few weeks later an Indian messenger brought a warning. "Run for your lives!" he shouted. "Massasoit and Canonicus are coming to attack. They have joined their tribes to drive out the white settlers. Run—."

The Pilgrims rushed from their houses. They could not believe their friend Massasoit would break their treaty. Captain Standish was ready to arm his men. Governor Bradford was more careful. "We will send scouts to see if there is really trouble," he said.

Before morning the scouts were back. "Massasoit's village is quiet," they said. "There is no sign of war."

Still the trouble was not over. Massasoit was very angry. He wanted to know who had sent the false warning. Hobomok said that Squanto had sent it.

Massasoit believed Squanto was guilty. He sent two of his braves to Plymouth. They gave Massasoit's knife to Governor Bradford. "Our chief says Squanto must be killed," they said. "We must take his head and hands back to Massasoit or there will be war."

Governor Bradford refused to give Squanto up. "Squanto must speak for himself," he said.

Squanto stood before the Governor and the council. "I am not guilty," he said.

The Pilgrims believed Squanto. "You cannot take him," they told the braves.

Before the Indians could answer, an alarm came from one of the guards at the shore. He had sighted a big ship off Manomet Point. The Pilgrims knew that French ships had been attacking English colonies. This might be a French attack.

"Get your guns," Captain Standish ordered the men. Some waited on the beach. Some went to the fort. They

fired a cannon in warning. Squanto took his station with the others.

When the ship showed the English flag, a cheer went up. It was a friendly fishing vessel.

Captain Standish and his men came back to the village. The Indian messengers were gone.

Chief Massasoit forgot his anger at Squanto. The Indians and the Pilgrims were friends again.

11

The Last Trip

All summer long, the Pilgrims waited for a supply ship. But none came.

Governor Bradford shook his head. "How will our food last out the winter? There are so many of us now."

The Pilgrims wanted corn from the Indians. But they had nothing left to trade.

November came. Soon the winter storms would begin.

One morning Squanto went out early to fish. He brought back good news. "An English ship is coming into the harbor," he said. "I called to the captain. He has a cargo of beads and knives and hatchets. We can trade our beaver skins for them."

Now the Pilgrims had new goods to trade with the Indians. "We will take our boat around Cape Cod and trade for Indian corn," Governor Bradford said. "There are dangerous shoals and tides, but Squanto will guide us."

They landed safely on Cape Cod. Squanto helped Captain Standish draw a map of the shore. The Nauset Indians had plenty of corn and beans to trade. Soon the Pilgrims' boat was loaded with food.

Squanto looked at the sky. "Good winds will take us home before the storms begin," he said.

That evening the men were roasting wild ducks and corn cakes for supper. The smell made them hungry.

Squanto sat by himself. He could not eat. His head ached. He felt hot with fever. He was restless all night.

In the morning, Squanto was very ill. His friends made a bed of pine boughs and covered him with coats. They kept the fire warm. They gave him water and herb tea to drink. Still his fever grew worse.

On the third day, Squanto asked Governor Bradford to pray that he would go to the same heaven as his English friends. He asked them to take his best knife back to Johnny. That night he died.

Squanto's life had been full of courage and adventure. Governor Bradford wrote the last words: *We have many remembrances of Squanto and his love for his friends. In his death they had a great loss.*